SCIENCE

Selected by
Robert Hull

Illustrated by
Annabel Spenceley

Wayland

Thematic Poetry

Animal Poetry
Christmas Poetry
Day and Night Poetry
Green Poetry
Science Poetry
Sea Poetry

Series editor: Catherine Ellis
Designer: Derek Lee

First Published in 1991 by
Wayland (Publishers) Ltd
61 Western Road, Hove
East Sussex BN3 1JD, England

© Copyright 1991 Wayland
(Publishers) Ltd

**British Library Cataloguing in
Publication Data**
Science poetry. – (Thematic poetry)
  I. Hull, Robert   II. Series
  821

  ISBN 0 7502 0223 8

Picture Acknowledgements
The publishers would like to thank
the following for allowing illustrations
to be reproduced in this book: Bruce
Coleman Ltd back cover (Jane
Burton), 8 (Dieter and Mary Plage),
23 (Hans Reinhard), 25 (Michael
Freeman), 30 (Gerald Cubitt), 42
(D. & J. McClurg); Tony Stone
Worldwide front cover; Topham
Picture Library 26; Zefa 5, 7, 11 (John
Flowerdew), 12 (Photo Research), 14,
19 (Photri), 21, 29 (Hackenberg), 33
(D. Cattani), 34 (N. Schafer), 37, 39,
41, 44.

Acknowledgements
For permission to reprint copyright
material the publishers gratefully
acknowledge the following: Cadbury Ltd
for 'Bubbles' by Ryan Goad and
'Electricity' by Rebecca Hughes from
*Cadbury's Eighth Book of Children's
Poetry*; Collins/Angus & Robertson for
'Observation' by William Hart-Smith from
Selected Poems 1936–84 © Estate of
William Hart-Smith 1985; John Foster for
'Facts about Air'; Katherine Gallagher for
'Song for an Unborn'; for two poems from
Miroslav Holub: Selected Poems (Penguin
Books, 1967), copyright © Miroslav
Holub, 1967, translation copyright ©
Penguin Books, 1967; Robert Hull for
'Galileo's Story'; Wes Magee for 'The
Buttercup Experiment'; Kevin McCann for
'A Science Lesson'; May Swenson for '3
Models of the Universe' © 1967 by May
Swenson and used with the permission of
the Literary Estate of May Swenson; Colin
West and Hutchinson for 'Etymology for
Entomologists' and 'Einstein' from *It's
Funny When You Look At It;* 'The Dinosaur
Bones' from *Good Morning, America*,
copyright 1928 and renewed 1956 by Carl
Sandburg, reprinted by permission of
Harcourt Brace Jovanovich, Inc; Leo Aylen
for 'The Whether Forecast'. While every
effort has been made to secure
permission, in some cases it has proved
impossible to trace the copyright holders.
The publishers apologise for this apparent
negligence.

Typeset by Kalligraphic Design Ltd,
Horley, Surrey
Printed in Italy by G. Canale &
C.S.p.A., Turin

Contents

Introduction		4
Electricity	*Rebecca Hughes*	6
A Fish	*Tom Stanier*	9
Observation	*W. Hart-Smith*	10
A Science Lesson	*Kevin McCann*	13
Bubbles	*Ryan Goad*	15
Communication	*Rob Morrison*	16
Song for an Unborn	*Katherine Gallagher*	18
Einstein	*Colin West*	20
The Whether Forecast	*Leo Aylen*	20
Facts About Air	*John Foster*	22
A Marvel	*Carolyn Wells*	24
The Dinosaur Bones	*Carl Sandburg*	27
The Forest	*Miroslav Holub*	28
(translated by George Theiner)		
The Purist	*Ogden Nash*	31
The Buttercup Experiment	*Wes Magee*	32
A Boy's Head	*Miroslav Holub*	35
(translated by Ian Milner)		
Crystals	*Barrie Wade*	36
Galileo's Story	*Robert Hull*	38
Whitman on Wheels	*Adrian Mitchell*	40
Etymology for Entomologists	*Colin West*	43
3 Models of the Universe	*May Swenson*	45
Biographies		46
Index of first lines		48

Introduction

If I came up to you in the classroom and said, 'Excuse me, are you a scientist?' you'd probably give one of those looks, and say, 'Of course not, I'm only at school! What a daft question!' But, it's the way you peer at frogspawn to see if the little dots have started wiggling that makes me think you're being a bit of a scientist. Especially when I see you write down your observations and put in the dates and times.

A boy once wrote this for me about snowballs: 'I saw something I had never noticed before; snowballs that had smashed against a wall had all taken up the same shape. They were like dead volcanoes with cold lava flows lining the slopes. Explanation: the same vibrations could have formed these shapes.' He was being a scientist by noticing the same shapes in all the smashed snowballs. But he was being a poet as well, seeing them as 'dead volcanoes'.

Poets and scientists have a lot in common. They both stand around just looking hard at things, to see what's really there. It's a special kind of concentrated day-dreaming. So it isn't surprising that some scientists are poets. One of the writers in this book, Miroslav Holub, is a world-famous poet and a world-famous scientist. He thinks science and poetry are alike. He says that seeing something unexpected in a microscope is just like seeing a new idea for a poem.

Of course ideas can be so new and unexpected they're hard to believe. When Galileo said he could see mountains on the moon, people said it was impossible. The moon was smooth, a perfect sphere. They said the 'mountains' were a trick of light that happened inside the tube of the telescope. Most of the time, though, new ideas come from seeing familiar things more clearly, in more detail. I listened to a crow in an oak tree recently. I thought they just cawed. Wrong. This crow was making strange, unexpected noises. I had to revise my ideas about crow-noise.

Try some concentrated day-dreaming for yourself. Count the different moods of water, how it behaves in different places. Follow the sparrow around to see exactly what it's up to. Listen to your friends in the playground to see if they make any strange, unexpected noises. If I watched you doing all this I'm sure I'd see a bit of a scientist starting to wiggle.

Electricity

I am electricity.
I go through the
land invisibly
into everything.

REBECCA HUGHES (Aged 5)

A Fish

A fish crawled out of the ocean
And flopped around in the sand:
And he told his friend
That the latest trend
Was amphibious life on land.
But his fishy friend was unconvinced;
He said that he couldn't agree.
He reckoned the shore
Was a bit of a bore
And he'd stay as a fish in the sea.

TOM STANIER

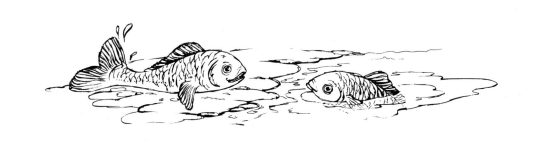

Observation

Now and then concentrating
on the very small,

focusing my attention
on a very small area

like this crack in sandstone
perpetually wet with seepage,

getting so close
to moss, liverwort, and fern

it becomes a forest . . .
with wild beasts in it

birds in the branches
and crickets piping,

cicadas shrilling.
Someone seeing me

staring so fixedly
at nothing

might be excused
for thinking me vague, abstracted,

lost in introspection.
No! I am awake, absorbed,

just looking in a different direction.

W. HART-SMITH

A Science Lesson

Look, here's fire.

Good, they all said.
Burn something.

Look here's the wheel.

Good, they all said.
Chariots.

Look, here's steel.

Good, they all said.
Keener blades.

Look, here's wings.

Good, they all said.
Air-raids.

Look, here's a necklace of atoms.

Good, they all said.
Whole cities shrivelling.

Look, here's space travel.

Good, they all said.
Star Wars.

Look, here's
Enough food,
Solar power,
A cure for cancer.

Liar, they all said.

KEVIN McCANN

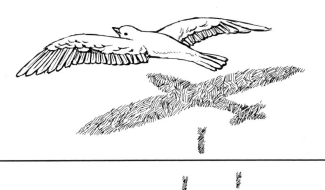

13

Bubbles

When you blow the
bubbles they wobble out
like fat rain floating sideways.
When you hold your hand out
sometimes they bounce up and
down until they fade away.
They look like a soft glass ball.
When they fall they leave behind water prints.
It looks like bubbles have got
windows with colours.
Green, purple, blue and white.
They float around looking wobbly and silvery.

RYAN GOAD (Aged 7)

Communication

My uncle is a scientist. He studied many years
To find out how the planets move, and whether flies have ears.
He dreams up new hypotheses. He learns the names of flowers.
He works out laws and theories. He calculates for hours.
I know that I'm not clever, but my uncle must be wise,
For when I ask short questions, I get very long replies.

I asked him if the sea is blue, for that is how it looks.
He put his glasses on and started looking through his books.
'The sea is colourless,' he said, 'the sun produces light,
And all the spectrum's colours are compounded into white.
But when the light is broken up, by sea or sky or rain,
The colours separate, and we can see the blue again.'

'Now which came first,' I said to him, 'the chicken or the egg?'
I thought it was a riddle. I was trying to pull his leg.
'The egg came first,' he said to me; 'that problem's quickly solved.
Reptilian dinosaurs lived long before the birds evolved,
And since the dinosaurs laid eggs – their fossils still persist –
The egg was there before the birds (or chickens) could exist.'

'But can you prove,' I asked him, 'that the earth is really round?'
'By round, do you mean, spherical?' he asked, and then he
    frowned.
'Imagine, if you will,' he said, 'a rubber tennis ball;
Now if you squeeze its top and base, it won't be round at all.
And that is how the earth appears when viewed from any side –
Elliptical, not spherical, and shorter than it's wide.'

'Then can you classify,' I asked, 'the bug that's in this tin?'
My uncle took the lid off, and he poked his finger in.
He pulled it out more quickly, and he gave a little shrug,
And said, 'The creature in this tin is *not* some kind of bug!
A bug must be six-legged. If this were, you could be right.
Instead it is a centipede, which has a painful bite!'

My uncle is a busy man. He seldom ever laughs.
He calculates equations and he draws elaborate graphs.
And sometimes he's so busy that he misses out on meals,
And writes me simple formulae to tell me how he feels.
'I C U R Y Y,' he writes, 'to skip your meals like me.
A P T I M B C, 4 I missed you'.

T

ROB MORRISON

Song for an Unborn

Child, curled in the night
I call you, know you
feeling your way against the walls.
You are so used to darkness now –
your blind busy limbs
buffet and push, quickening
as you weigh yourself and float.

In the beginning, I ran through hours
trying to feel you real.
Daily I bargained with you,
was cajoled and soothed
by your moves, winning,
always teaching me. And yesterday
you set yourself on X-ray, vividly
thumb in mouth, head down, a plunderer
looping in the sky.

Half-afraid with new happiness
I scanned that picture,
hunting details – your face, body,
you. Suddenly I knew
your eyes were almost ready
to lift the dark.

KATHERINE GALLAGHER

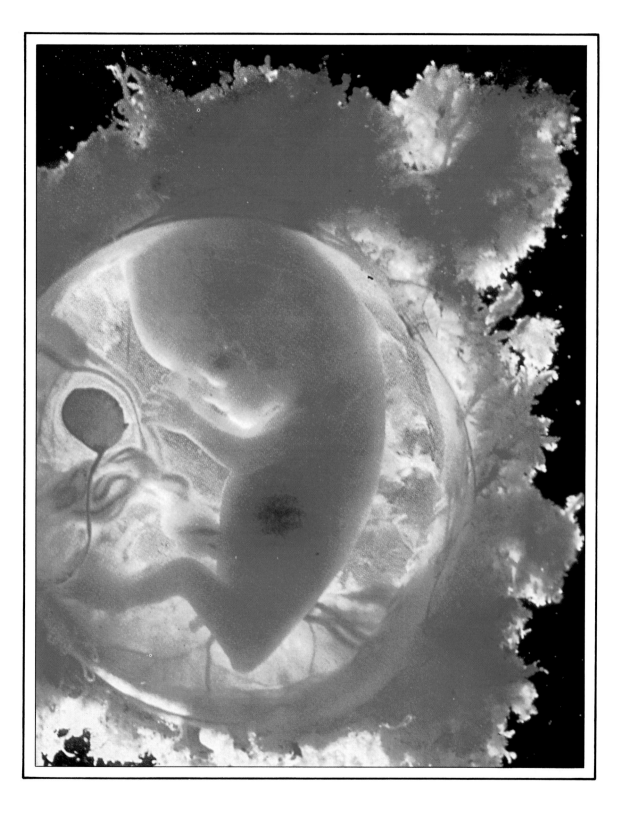

19

Einstein

Long years ago, nobody cared
That E was really mc^2.
Then Albert Einstein thought a bit,
And felt that he should mention it.

COLIN WEST

The Whether Forecast

'This is the Whether Forecast.
I don't know whether it will rain or not.'

LEO AYLEN

Facts about Air

Scientists say
That air consists
Of about 78% nitrogen and 21% oxygen,
Plus some carbon dioxide
And small amounts
Of the rare gases – helium, argon and neon.

These are facts, I know.
But I also know
That when I go outside
On a spring morning
The air tastes as crisp
As a fresh lettuce
And that when I sit
On the patio
On a summer evening
The cool night air
Brushes my cheeks like a feather.

JOHN FOSTER

A Marvel

An old astronomer there was
  Who lived up in a tower;
Named Ptolemy Copernicus
  Flammarion McGower.
He said: 'I can prognosticate
  With estimates correct;
And when the skies I contemplate,
  I know what to expect.
When dark'ning clouds obscure my sight,
  I think perhaps 'twill rain;
And when the stars are shining bright,
  I know 'tis clear again.'
And then abstractedly he scanned
  The heavens, hour by hour,
Old Ptolemy Copernicus
  Flammarion McGower.

CAROLYN WELLS

The Dinosaur Bones

The dinosaur bones are dusted every day.
The cards tell how old we guess the dinosaur bones are.
Here a head was seven feet long, horns with a hell of a ram,
Humping the humps of the Montana mountains.
        The respectable school children
Chatter at the heels of their teacher who explains.
The tourists and wonder hunters come with their parasols
And catalogues and arrangements to do the museum
In an hour or two hours.
        The dinosaur bones
          are dusted
          every day.

CARL SANDBURG

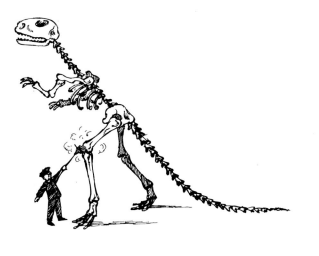

The Forest

Among the primary rocks
where the bird spirits
crack the granite seeds   and there grows
and the tree statues
with their black arms   a mushroom,
threaten the clouds,

                                 immense as life itself,
suddenly   filled with billions of cells
there comes a rumble,   immense as life itself,
as if history   eternal,
were being uprooted,   watery,

the grass bristles,   appearing in this world for the first
boulders tremble,
the earth's surface cracks   and last time.

MIROSLAV HOLUB
(Translated from the Czechoslovakian
by George Theiner)

The Purist

I give you now Professor Twist,
A conscientious scientist.
Trustees exclaimed, 'He never bungles!'
And sent him off to distant jungles.
Camped on a tropic riverside,
One day he missed his loving bride.
She had, the guide informed him later,
Been eaten by an alligator.
Professor Twist could not but smile.
'You mean,' he said, 'a crocodile.'

OGDEN NASH

The Buttercup Experiment

From the overgrown lawn I picked a buttercup
and held it under my sister's chin.
'This is the buttercup experiment,' I said,
'let's see if it shines yellow on your skin.'

It did. 'It means you like butter.'
We gathered more buttercups. The day was hot.
On the kitchen window-sill we arranged them
in a plastic beaker and a yoghurt pot.

How they glowed . . . like little suns,
or butter on toast, or flame of candlelight!
So much brighter than the dullness of mustard
or the moon's pale face on a dark winter's night.

WES MAGEE

A Boy's Head

In it there is a space-ship
and a project
for doing away with piano lessons.

And there is
Noah's ark,
which shall be first.

And there is
an entirely new bird,
an entirely new hare,
an entirely new bumble-bee.

There is a river
that flows upwards.

There is a multiplication table.

There is anti-matter.

And it just cannot be trimmed.

I believe
that only what cannot be trimmed
is a head.

There is much promise
in the circumstance
that so many people have heads.

MIROSLAV HOLUB
(Translated from the Czechoslovakian
by Ian Milner)

35

Crystals

First, in saucers we spread salt.
Our imagination turns

its shimmer into spoil heaps
drawn from far-off diamond mines

beneath the tawny plain
of Africa. We hold this dream

until the drench of water
vanquishes their fire.

A string of disappearing pools,
we range them along windowsills

and the sun steals in on lion's paws
to lap away their drink.

Our teacher mixes 'poison'
in a glass apart for safety;

it attracts us like a blinding sky
of fierce, ice-shattering blue.

Our waterholes days later
have dried up to brittle crusts

of sharp-edged crystals
glittering like splintered glass.

Ice-wonder fills our eyes
almost to snow-blinding.

Our teacher's soft brown hand
shows diamonds of blue

deeper than sky or sea.
Her eyes sparkle ice and fire.

BARRIE WADE

Galileo's Story

Galileo
Galilei
from Italy
invented seeing

a long way
and believing it.
He invented mountains
on the moon

and a lot of stars
that were further off
than the others.
He invented

leaning
over the leaning
tower of Pisa
and saying here's a

big one coming down
and a little one
going the same speed
just you see.

He worked harder and harder
and got ill
so he invented
taking your temperature.

Before long
he'd invented
being right too often
when important

people were wrong
and had to invent
pretending to have
second thoughts

and important people
being right again.
His enemies'
only invention

was putting him
in prison
in his own home
when he was an old man

in case he did
any more damage
to their best
ancient ideas.

ROBERT HULL

Whitman on Wheels

Fanfare: in transports over transport
I salute all passenger-carrying machines –
The admirable automobile, the glottal motor-cycle,
The womby capsule bound for Mars,
The tube train (see how well it fits its tube),
The vibrant diesel, The Little Engine That Could
And all manner of aeroplanes whether they carry
Hostesses, hogs or horror,
Gargantuan traction engines,
Curmudgeonly diggers, bull-dozers, dinosauric tank-tracked
    cranes,
Zoomers, splutterers, purrers and gliders
I salute you all,
And also the reliable tricycle.

ADRIAN MITCHELL

41

Etymology for Entomologists

O Longitude and Latitude,
I always get them muddled;
(I'm sure they'd be offended, though,
To think that I'm befuddled).

O Isobars and Isotherms,
Please tell me how they differ;
(For competition 'twixt the two,
I hear, could not be stiffer).

O Seraphim and Cherubim,
Don't care for one another;
(Although for me it's difficult
To tell one from the other).

O Stalagmites and Stalactites,
Whenever I peruse 'em,
Though one grows up, and one grows down,
I can't help but confuse 'em.

COLIN WEST

3 Models of the Universe

1 At moment X
   the universe began.
   It began at point X.
   Since then,
   through the Hole in a Nozzle,
   stars have spewed. An
   inexhaustible gush
   populates the void forever.

2 The universe was there
   before time ran.
   A grain
   slipped in the glass:
   the past began.
   The Container
   of the Stars expands;
   the sand
   of matter multiplies forever.

3 From zero radius
   to a certain span,
   the universe, a Large Lung
   specked with stars,
   inhales time
   until, turgent, it can
   hold no more,
   and collapses. Then
   space breathes, and inhales again,
   and breathes again: Forever.

MAY SWENSON

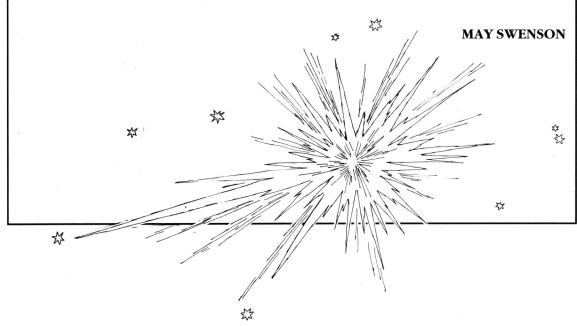

Biographies

Leo Aylen was born in Zululand and studied at Oxford and Bristol. He has read his work on American television and on British television and radio. He has worked as a writer in residence on both sides of the Atlantic, in New York, in Ontario, and in Lambeth, London.

John Foster has been a teacher and a school headteacher. As well as writing poetry for children he has compiled several anthologies, written books about teaching, and worked on radio and television.

Katherine Gallagher is an Australian who has lived in London since 1979. She has published four books of poems. The most recent is *Fish-Rings on Water*, published by Forest Books in 1989. She writes poems for children and holds poetry workshops in schools.

Ryan Goad was seven, and a pupil at Lincewood Junior School, Basildon, when he wrote 'Bubbles' for the 1990 Cadbury Poetry Competition.

William Hart-Smith was born in Tunbridge Wells in 1911, and emigrated to New Zealand in 1924. He went from there to Australia in 1936. He has worked as clerk to a shipping company, radio mechanic and serviceman, and radio announcer. He has written eleven books of poetry.

Rebecca Hughes was five when she wrote 'Electricity', which won a Silver Medal Award in the 1990 Cadbury Poetry Competition. She was then at St. Catherine's School, Camberley, in Surrey.

Robert Hull was a schoolteacher for twenty-five years. He has written several books for children and *Behind the Poem*, a book about children writing poetry. Some of his poems were published in *Peterloo Preview 2*, and an anthology of his poetry, *Encouraging Shakespeare*, will be published by Peterloo in 1992.

Kevin McCann was born in Widnes but grew up in Blackpool. He has written poems for as long as he can remember and has published two books for adults. He worked for twelve years as a teacher, but is now a professional writer. At present he is writing a book of poems for children.

Wes Magee lives in Yorkshire. He is a full-time writer, who started writing for adults and went on to write many books for children. His recent book, *Morning Break*, was voted one of the best children's books of 1989.

Adrian Mitchell was born in London in 1932. He was educated at Oxford, and became a reporter, TV and radio playwright, poet and novelist. He has written two books of poems for adults, and his children's poems are collected in *Nothingmas Day*, illustrated by John Lawrence.

Robert Morrison was born in 1915 in Australia, and later attended the University of Melbourne. He has written several volumes of poetry, and is very well known as an anthologist and translator of poetry.

Ogden Nash is perhaps the best-known writer of comic verse in the USA. He has been called 'the funniest poet this country has known'.

Carl Sandburg was an American writer who lived from 1878 to 1967. After leaving school he wandered round the Midwest, then went as a soldier to Puerto Rico to fight in the Spanish-American War. He wrote many stories and poems for children. They're collected in a beautiful book called *The Sandburg Treasury*.

May Swenson was born in 1919 in Utah. Her parents were Swedish, and she has translated Swedish poetry into English. She has published many books of poems for adults, and three for children: *Poems to Solve, More Poems to Solve*, and *The Guess and Spell Colouring Book*.

Barrie Wade was born in Derbyshire and taught in schools before becoming senior lecturer in education at the University of Birmingham. He has written stories and poetry for radio, and has won prizes in the National Poetry Competition. His first book of poetry for children, *Conkers*, was published in 1989.

Carolyn Wells (1862–1942) wrote about 170 books. She was born in New Jersey, USA, and wrote detective novels, and comic verse.

Colin West was born in 1951. He studied illustration at the Royal College of Art. He has written or illustrated more than thirty children's books and is now a full-time writer/illustrator. He visits schools with his one-man show, which includes 'tongue-twisters and lightning sketches'.

Index of first lines

A fish crawled out of the ocean	**9**
Among the primary rocks	**28**
An old astronomer there was	**24**
At moment X	**45**
Child, curled in the night	**18**
Fanfare: in transports over transport	**40**
First, in saucers we spread salt.	**36**
From the overgrown lawn I picked a buttercup	**32**
Galileo	**38**
I am electricity.	**6**
I give you now Professor Twist,	**31**
In it there is a space-ship	**35**
Long years ago, nobody cared	**20**
Look, here's fire.	**13**
My uncle is a scientist. He studied many years	**16**
Now and then concentrating	**10**
O Longitude and Latitude,	**43**
Scientists say	**22**
The dinosaur bones are dusted every day.	**27**
'This is the Whether Forecast.	**20**
When you blow the	**15**